How to Speak
DUTCH-ified
ENGLISH

Volume 2 (TWOAH)

How to Speak
DUTCH-ified
ENGLISH

Volume 2 (TWOAH)

GARY GATES

Drawings by KEVIN GATES

Good Books

Intercourse, PA 17534

Design by Dawn J. Ranck

HOW TO SPEAK DUTCH-IFIED ENGLISH, Wolume 2 (Twoah)
Copyright © 1998 by Gary Gates
International Standard Book Number: 1-56148-243-9
Library of Congress Catalog Card Number: 87-82012

Library of Congress Cataloging-in-Publication Data

Gates, Gary.
    How to speak Dutch-ified English / Gary Gates;
drawings by Kevin Gates
            96 p. : ill. ; 19cm.
    ISBN: 1-56148-243-9

    1. English language—Dialects—Pennsylvania.
2. Pennsylvania Dutch—Languages. 3. Pennsylvania
German dialect—Influence. 4. English language—Foreign
elements—German. I. Title. II. Title: Dutchified English.
PE3102.P45G3 1987 427'.9748—dc19   87-82012
                                        AACR 2 MARC

Taple uff Cuntents

Right hereah, on dis paitch

Dedication

This book is gratefully dedicated to the thousands of people who have helped me make *How to Speak Dutch-ified English, Wolume Vun* a success. Thank you for your letters and for sharing your Dutch-ified humor with me wherever I have traveled throughout Pennsylvania Dutch country. I hope many of you will recognize your contributions to this book.

Thanks to you, this *Wolume Twoah* contains elements of Dutch-ified English from all areas of Dutch-ified America, helping to make this book much broader in its Dutchiness than *Wolume Vun.*

Preface

Why do so many people spend so much time trying to speak as if they come from nowhere?

For myself, I'm proud to speak as if I come from somewhere. I come from Pennsylvania Dutch country, and I enjoy the way we speak around here.

Since **How to Speak Dutch-ified English, Wolume Vun** was published, many people have become a little more proud and a little less ashamed of the way they speak. And many people who have migrated to this area, or who have just passed through, have picked up some of our flavorful words, expressions, and pronunciations.

The effect of **How to Speak Dutch-ified English, Wolume Vun** has been profound. People who once dreaded the subject of English now enjoy it! It has been said that to truly understand one's native tongue, one should learn a foreign language, one should understand at least one, even several, regional Englishes.

There are people who say that regional Englishes ought to be overcome, that they are bad English. I believe that English is powerful precisely because of all its variety. Just imagine going to Ireland and not hearing an Irish brogue. Or going to Scotland and not hearing a brrrrr of the tongue. Or being in the South and not hearing any good ol' boys bantering in

Southern. Just imagine if everyone everywhere spoke like Tom Brokaw. How dull.

In France there is an institute to protect the purity of the French language. They try to prevent foreign words and expressions from corrupting French. Fine. Let the French isolate their language from the complex and changing world and all its many cultural impacts. They will likely stultify their language and kill it off, going the way of Latin.

English is alive. It grows and changes every day. It takes in words from this ethnic group and that ethnic group. Not only do many cultural groups learn English, they also contribute to English and change it for the better. Every strand and fiber borrowed from other tongues make the majestic fabric of English stronger, more beautiful, more intricately laden with design and meaning.

Native Americans, Yiddish-speaking Jews, Hispanics, African-Americans, Europeans, Southerners, Valley Girls, Bostonians, jargon-users, jive cats, technocrats, and most of the ethnic groups of the word have all helped make American English the most inclusive language on the face of the earth.

Dutch-ified English has made, and is more and more making, its own unique impact on the English language. It is one of the most humorous and delightful varieties of English. It is full of humor, insight, and the power to make common and dull matters take on a hilarious dimension.

A lawyer friend of mine has been buying multiple copies of **How to Speak Dutch-ified English, Wolume Vun** for his clients to read while they wait, because they keep stealing every copy he puts out. One day a couple came into his office who were mad at each other and intent on obtaining a divorce. While they fumed in the waiting room, the husband picked up a copy of *How to Speak Dutch-ified English, Wolume Vun.* He started to chuckle. His wife came over to see what was so funny. Soon they were laughing together. When they finished reading the book, they left hand in hand, laughing, their divorce forgotten.

Many other strange and wonderful things have happened. Choirs have started singing in Dutch-ified English, much to the delight of congregations everywhere. Hospitals sell copies to patients, and, through the laughter the book generates, recovery rates have improved markedly. The ill have been healed, the depressed lifted, the gloomy enlightened, the divorced brought back together, all by the power of Dutch-ified English.

This has led to a movement to make Dutch-ified English the language into which the United Nations will translate all their speeches. Imagine it. No matter what anyone would say, no matter how belligerent they would become, when their speech was rendered in Dutch-ified English, all members would crack up laughing. There would be no more war, no more strife between the nations. Peace would finally come to our planet.

English is not a subject to be approached with serious dread. It is the medium, best expressed through Dutch-ified English, that can cheerfully change your life. So save your marriage, heal yourself, cut down on the strife and disharmony in your life.

If you're already happy, practice and talk this variety of English wherever you go. People will stop in their tracks and look at you in amazement. They will talk and murmur among themselves, "What is this strange and wonderful thing? Is it French?" Then you can tell them and teach them about Dutch-ified English, all in an effort to help make the world a more fun and enjoyable place.

Then we will all talk like we come from somewhere wunst. Somewhere wonderful good.

Dictionary
of Terms

In the Dictionary section of this book are sentences using only one, or a few, Dutch-ified words, so that the featured word is evident and the contextual meaning clear.

Inevitably, varieties result. This is as it should be since diversity abounds in Dutch-ified English. Many regional enclaves of German-Dutch settlers throughout the United States and Canada, often heavily populated by the Amish and Mennonites, have their own varieties of Dutch-ified English. The localities, cities, and towns within each region have their own sub-varieties. In Pennsylvania, people in Lancaster speak a form of Dutch-ified English different than that found in Lebanon or Reading. However, there is a common thread to all of them.

The more people distance themselves from their German-Dutch heritage, the less pronounced is their Dutch-ified English. But in distancing themselves from their roots, they create their own unique, individualized version of Dutch-ified English. An influence always remains!

A

Abhorse: Hates. "The boss abhorse Sam, because he's so lazy."

Abuff: Not below. "I won't sink to that level. I'm abuff it."

Ach Du Lieber: Oh my goodness. "Ach du lieber! He didn't!"

Addick: The upper room. "We rummaged through the old stuff up in the addick."

After: Redd up the haus. "She's so busy she just can't keep after."

Against: Went up to. "I went up against him and asked him to his face." Also: "Mom was gonna hang out the wash today but the weather was against her."

Ago: In the past. "It was ago when it happened."

Ah Wire: A French term said in parting. "Ah Wire! Enchoy your trip!"

Aislelent: A plot of grawnd surrawnded by water. "A lot of aislelents were formed by wolcanos."

Al: A nocturnal bird; a contraction of the personal pronoun; a space you walk down between chairs. "Mom! Look at the al up in the tree! It's hooting, too!" Also: "Yes, Al come with." Also: "When you walk down that al, you'll come back hitched."

Alblum: A large record; a book of photographs. "Sadie's always pasting pictures in the alblum."

Allah: Permit. "Are you allahed?"

Altar: An older person. "Elmer is an altar in the church."

Annwill: What a blacksmith hammers on. "Silas is hammering the horseshoe on the annwill."

Ape: A distinguished name. "The 16th President was Ape."

Around: Up. "Go get dressed around. The party's soon." Also: "Let's go walk the block around."

Arras: Shafts shot from bows. "Ach! To risk the slinks and arras of outrageous fortune!"

Arser: A harmless drudge, a compiler of words. "The arser of this book sure has lots of fun with it."

Aside Of: Better than beside. "Anatasia sits aside of her friend in school."

Arthuritis: Inflammation of the joints. "Hilary is in bet with arthuritis."

Atwertice: Proclaim for sale. "If you want to increase your sales, you have to atwertice."

Awhile: While you wait. "Can I get you some water awhile?"

Awoid: Keep away from. "Some things should be awoided."

Awsentic: Chenuwine. "Is that document awsentic?"

Awitch: An electrical failure. "We didn't have any lights after the thunderstorm. There was a par awtich."

Awtraychous: Crazy, bizarre. "There go those slinks and arras of awtrachous fortune again!"

Ape Lincoln

Aye Yi Yi: An expression of surprise, sometimes of disgust. "Aye yi yi! You silly boy!"

B

Back Dawn Through: Go there. "Let's go back down through and have a picnic wunst."

Backwards: A creatively used word. "Peter's going so wonderful fast backwards in his mind." Also: "It comes so backwards out."

Bar: Loan. "Go over to the neighbors and bar a cup of sugar."

Barkin: Something cheap. "Sometimes at yard sales you can find some real good barkins."

Barn Raising: When all the members of a community get together to help raise a barn for a less fortunate member who has lost his; a way to turn misfortune and work into a party.

Bawnd: Destined. "With my collitch decree, I'm bawnd to succeed."

Beefer: An aquatic mammal. "He's as busy as a beefer."

Bellsnickle: A costumed prankster who came around at Christmastime.

Bench: Short for Benchamin. "Franklin's parents called him Bench."

Beppy Bhumer: A member of the beppy bhum. "Yes, I'm a beppy bhumer."

Picking a Bookie

Berts: Feathered animals that fly. "My uncle is an avid bert-watcher."

Bic: Not little. "Your son sure is bic!" Also: "Michener wrote bic books."

Bip: A cloth worn to protect a diner's shirt. "Do you wear a bip when you eat lobster?"

Bips: What kids say when they want a share of something. "Bips! I want some Pez, too. Bips!"

Blabbermaul: A talkative person. "The blabbermaul has a phone bill you wouldn't believe."

Blace: Location. "Your blace or my blace?"

Bletch: Spank. "You keep that up and you get bletched!"

Blowny: A type of lunchmeat. "Lepnin has a Blowny Fest to celebrate its famous blowny." Also blonah. "My wife, Alice, went to Blownah, Italy, to study cooking."

Blutz: Pothole; a jolt or bruise. "My car needs a front-end alignment. It's hit one too many blutzens." Also: "My wife hit me on the arm and gave me a good blutz."

Bollixed Up: Ferhoodled. "Why, the modern world's enough to bollix anybody up."

Boofay: A spread of foods. "Get your plate and help yourself to the boofay."

Bookie: Nose gook. "Ugh! Alexander ate his bookie!"

Boomer: Storm. "Close the windows! A boomer's coming!"

Boopy: Infant. "It's time to feed boopy."

Booger up: Mess up. "If you don't know what you're doing, don't booger it up."

Booze: A stand where something is sold. "Adam worked in a booze at the street fair wunst."

Bot Boy: Pot pie. "Give me a plate of bot boy, please."

Both: Either. "A man looking for his dog said to his friend: 'Now you go up one side of the crick, and I'll go up the other. You know, he may come back both sides.'"

Bought the Farm: Died. "Harold isn't yet. He bought the farm."

Boygraut: Pie plant, i.e. Rhubarb. "Go pull some boy-graut."

Bratwurst: Fried pork sausitch. "Is that bratwurst in your sandvich?"

Breeze: Inhale and exhale. "Is he dead yet? Put a feather under his nose and see if he's still breezing." Also: "Breeze deeply!"

Brick: Jag, poke. "Sarah bricked her finger on the rosebush!"

Bruce: A welt, sore. "Bill's got a bruce on his arm."

Brum: What you sweep with. "Go out and brum off the sidewalk."

Buck: Necessary pests. "Listen to those bucks being electrocuted in the buck zapper!"

Bull Banding: Noise made by revelers to disturb honeymooners until they come out and feed them.

Bump: Knock. "If the doorbell don't make, bump."

Bun Bun: A chocolate candy. "Isaac gave his sweetheart some bun buns for Walentine's Day."

Bun Mot: A clever remark. "Us Dutchies know some pretty goot bun mots, ain't?"

Bun Woyitch: What you say to someone when they're going on a journey, especially if by ship. "Bun Woyitch! See you in September!"

Burny: Hot. "Mexican food is too burny for her to eat."

Burpin: A type of whiskey. "Paul prefers Scotch to burpin in his soda."

Bus: Kiss. "Give your mom a bus."

Butt: A baby flar. "Look at the butt on the rose! It's so pretty!"

C

Catch Flies: Yawn; doze. "Pop's on the porch catching flies."

Caw Tipping: A nocturnal sport whereby players attempt to knock over sleeping caws. "Have you ever tried caw tipping?"

Cease: Grab hold of. "Cease the day!"

Census: Marbles; perceptions. "He acts like he's lost his census."

Cha: Affirmative; food. "Cha. Dat's right." Also: "It's time to cha dawn!" Also: Italian for good-bye: "Cha!"

Chain: A woman's name. "Tarzan would swing through the trees with his Chain hanging on his back."

Cheese, That's a Big Buck!

Char: A glass container. "Take a pickle out of the char."

Char Lit: The top of a glass container. "Before you can take out the pickle, you have to make the lit off."

Cheans: Plew trawsers. "In the summer we wear cut-off cheans."

Cheese Viss: An expression of surprise. "Cheese Viss! Ain't that something now!"

Cheese 'N Grackers: Something you say to let off steam. "Cheese 'n grackers dat was a close call!"

Cheesus: The son of Got. "Some people go to church to worship Cheeses."

Cheeses Boom: An expression of surprise. "Cheesus boom! I didn't know that!"

Chest: Joke. "Esau always did enjoy a good chest."

Chet: A kind of airplane. "Amy flew to Rome on a chet." Also: "Are you a member of the chet set?"

Chet Lack: What you get after you fly on a chet. "After she got to Rome, Amy suffered from chet lack."

Chew: An Issraeli. "My best friend is a Chew."

Chews: What comes out of squeezed fruit. "I want some oranch chews."

Chew the Speck: Talk aimlessly. "When they get together they chust chew the speck."

Chick: Hip, cool. "That dress is really chick."

Chin: A kind of liquor. "You put some chin in a martini." Also: a machine for processing cotton. "Who invented the cotton chin?"

Christkindling: At Christmas, an event when young people with blackened faces would wish neighbors Merry Christmas and Happy New Year in verse.

Choon: A month. "We were married in Choon."

Chuly: Another woman's name. "My parents were going to name my sister Viola, but they were afraid the neighbors would call her Wiola. So they named her Chuly instead. Chuly. You know, like Chuly Nixon."

Clawn: A funny person. "Naw knock it off, you clawn!"

Clue: Sticky stuff; adhesive. "David can't fix your chair chust yet. He's out of clue."

Cluecumper: An unpicked pickle. "Are these cluecumpers in the salad?"

Cluttering up: Gathering. "It's cluttering up for a boomer!"

Cot: Have. "Hey! Watcha cot?"

Cran: What kids color with. "Jacob got a new box of crans for his birthday, and those crans have some wonderful pretty colors in them like I've never seen before."

Crap: A marine crustacean. "Sometimes we drive all the way to the shore just to eat fresh craps." Also: "I enjoy Alaskan King crap."

Crapcakes: Cakes made from fresh crap. "Fry up some crapcakes."

Crass: Green stuff that grows in your yard. "Time to cut the crass!"

Craut: A bunch of people. "You can pick him out in a craut."

Crash Helmet: Bonnet. "Are you going to wear your new crash helmet to church?"

Crate: Better than good. "Mom! Today in school we learned all about Alexander the Crate!"

Cratiate: Pass; move on to higher things. "Mary finally cratiated from the uniwersity."

Crave: What someone is buried in. "Where are your parents' craves?" Also: "You're digging your own crave."

Crouch: A person who gripes. "He's chust an old crouch."

Croshries: What you buy at the croshry story. "Why it costs a body a small fortune to buy croshries for a family anymore."

Cruce: A trip on a ship. "There's nothing like a good cruce."

Cruddled Milk: Milk gone sour.

Cunfrinse: Get-together to talk. "Let's have a cunfrinse."

Cup: A baby animal. "The lioness just delivered four cups." Also: "My son chust choined the Cup Scawts."

D

Daw Chones: A stock affritch. "Iss the Daw Chones up or dawn yet?"

Diesel Fitter: What parents say at crotch sales when they find some clothing that will fit their daughter. "Vy look, Pop, diesel fitter!"

Different Ones: Several people. "Different ones have told me it's so!"

Dippy Doppy: To goof arawnd. "One night we had nothing to do so we chust dippy doppied arawnd tawn."

Discos: What fits. "Discos over here or datcos over there."

Discumbuperated: Upset; confused. "After he was spun around a couple of times, he got all discumbuperated."

Distlefink: A fantastical bird found mostly in Pennsylvania Dutch hex signs.

Ditcha: Really? Are you sure? "Ach, naw, ditcha?"

Ditchit: A single number; a finger. "One is a single ditchit."

Do: Perform labor. "Well, I've got to go to work and do."

Dop up: Soak up. "Dop up that gravy with your bread."

Dopple: An awkward person. "Ken's such a dopple."

Dotter: Female offspring. "Anna is my dotter."

Dough: Even if. "It's not easy, dough." Also: "Will you love me even dough?"

Drissle: To make down lightly; spritz. "Why it's not so bad. We can still go. It's only drissling awt."

Dry Dings: Dried apples. "Do you like to eat dry dings?" Also: "You can't bob for dry dings."

Duff: The bird of peace. "Maybe our national bird shouldn't be an eagle but a duff." Also: "The cooing of duffs in the morning is a common sound."

Dunna Wedder: A mild curse, literally thunder weather. "Ach! Dunna wedder. We can't go on the picnic now yet. It's raining still."

Dunnerhead: Dumbkopf. "What for are you going, you Dunnerhead?"

Duss: Accomplishes. "What duss he do for a living?" "He duss?"

E

Earp: A small plant used in seasoning. "She keeps an earp garden. She likes to put fresh earps on her food."

Earl: The thing on the roof that gives good T-Wee. "Can you adjust the earl? The picture's not in right."

Easy: At least. "How long is it? Why it's an hour, easy."

Eats good: Tastes good. "Dat snitz and gnepp sure eats good."

Ebel Boy: Apple pie. "Eat a piece of ebel boy." Also: Ed's as American as ebel boy."

Effer: Always. "I want to be with you for effer and effer."

Ei Ei Ei: Another way of saying "aye yi yi."

Ellum: A kind of tree. "Don't cut down that ellum!"

Empahr: A united group of nations or companies. "Cyrus created the Persian Empahr." Also: "Did you ever climb the Empahr State Building?"

Endie: A female uncle. "Give your endie a buss!"

Entrinse: Where you go in. "There was a line at the entrinse."

Engines: The first Americans. "When Columbus arrived, he found the New World full of Engins." Also: "The fort was attacked by Engines."

Era: Mistake. "When a ballplayer misses a catch, he makes an era."

Esstensiff: Thorough, complete. "The course is esstensiff."

Et: Fed yourself. "Have you et yet?"

Eyes: Frozen water. "Don't skate on the eyes, it's awful thin." Also: "Put those trays in the freezer and make some eyes."

F

Fal: A tool used to smooth rough edges; unpleasant; birds. "Is that a wood fal or a metal fal?" Also: "What's that fal odor?" Also: "A duck is a water fal."

Fall Off the Roof: Menstruate. "Don't talk to her now. She just fell off the roof."

False: Come down. "Did you ever go to the Niagra False?"

Fartzich: Forty. "Congratulations! Here's to another fartzich years!"

Fate: Pass away; become dull. "The General was so dynamic when he was young. But now that he's older he's beginning to fate." Also: "The sun is causing the colors in the picture to fate."

Fawrest: A big voods. "Robin Hoot lived in Shervood Fawrest."

Feel Your Nerve: Be ashamed. "That's terrible! You should feel your nerve!"

Fendue Groyer: Auctioneer. "Can you make awt what the fendue groyer says?"

Ferflooched: Cursed. "Dracula was ferflooched."

Fershimmled: Confused. "The modern world makes some people fershimmled."

Fersummling: A Dutch-ified gathering with a meal, song, and story-telling, with only Pennsylvania German allowed to be spoken throughout.

Feudal: Not productive. "Some people think it's feudal to try to change the world."

Fillum: What pictures are shot on; moofies. "Where do you get your fillum deweloped?" Also: "We enchoy watching old fillums."

Fip: A white lie. "Naw don't tell me anymore fips."

Fire Buck: Lightning buck. "A char uff fire bucks iss a natchral lantern."

Fleas: Sheep wool. "His fleas was white as snow." Also: "Look at the fleas on that sheep!"

Flars: Pretty things that grow on stems. "Abril shars bring May flars."

Flitch: Do it up quickly. "Flitch that project, man. We need it yesterday."

Flitch-Flatches: Bacon. "Nothing like the smell of sizzling flitch-flatches to get you up in the morning."

Flock: Whip. "In the old British Navy, they would flock sailors if they were out of line." Also: "The mutineers were flocked."

Flutz: Pollute. "Your car's flutzin' up the air!"

Force: Come out of. "Our forefathers brought force on this continent . . ."

Fond it Missing: Lost it. "I was out of money when I fond my wallet missing."

Fount: Past tense of fond. "I wunst was lost, but now I'm fount."

Fraktur: Old German handwriting.

Fress: Eat heartily; overeat. "You can't dichest your food properly if you fress." Also: "I feel like a fressen pig."

Fresserei: Picnic, cookout. "What a beautiful day for a fresserei!"

Fright: Boiled or cooked in oil or grease; burned, ruined. "Do you like your fish broiled or fright?" Also: "He drank so much so long his brain was fright."

Frissen: Fixing. "I must make an appointment for a good hair frissen."

Fritch: Ice box. "Fetch me a sota frum the fritch, Mom."

Front: Town. "Come front and see the new Christmas decorations."

Fussy: Not clear. "The picture's a little fussy. Can you focus it?"

G

Gabootz: Clean. "You can't leave the table until you make your plate gabootz."

Gakutz: Vomit. "The Romans used to have gakutztitoriums!"

Gap: Talk. "That woman can sure gap."

Gawkies: X. "Do you like your gawkies dippy style?"

Gay: To deny one's Pennsylvania Dutchiness. "John tries to hide his accent ever since he went gay."

Geh: Ain't that so. "You come from up the road, geh?"

Get: Come out. "If you don't have enough light, the picture won't get."

Get Your Pig: See "Fall Off the Roof."

Giff: Agree with. "I giff you right."

Giggee: Rear end. "He's a pain up the giggee."

Glock: Timepiece. "We're gonna rock arawnd the glock tonight."

Go Back Down Arawnd Through: A long way of putting it. "Let's go back down arawnd through, and then when we get there, we can talk a little after."

Go Out: Go to the restroom (outhouse). Woman to a store clerk: "I came in to go out. Do you have such a place?"

Gook: Sticky stuff found on the bottom of a shoo-fly pie; any sticky, gooey stuff. "Put some gook on that axle so it'll turn better." Also: "This gook tastes wonderful good!"

Gookies: Eyes. "When I looked into her gookies, I fell in love."

Goose-Pimply: Cold. "I'm not goose-pimply all over yet."

Goxy: Funny looking. "Some people sure are goxy."

Grate: A wooden box. "Pack those oranges in that grate."

Groan: On the grow. "My son sure is groan."

Gross: Past tense of grow. "After a good rain, the corn sure gross."

Guleraus: Turkey. "Vhy noah. Ve eat guleraus at Thanksgiving."

H

Hahr: Employ. "Do you think they'll hahr me?"

Hairs: Plural of hair. "Go get your hairs cut." "Becky has pretty hairs."

Hampburker Meat: The all-American food. "Does McDunult's use hampburker meat in their hampburkers, do you think?"

Hawana: The capital of Cupa. "Castro lives in Hawana."

Hearse: Not his. "Is this hearse?" "Yes, that purse is hearse."

Heinty: Rear end. "You're gonna get spanked on your heinty!"

Herschel: Storm or sudden change in the weather. "Close the windows! A herschel's coming!"

Hex: Spell. "That old pow-wow doctor will put a hex on you."

Hexerei: Witchcraft. "Be careful. Rebecca's smile is something like hexerei."

Hinches: Door fasteners. "Put the door back on its hinches."

Hind: At the end of. "Halloween's at the hind part of October."

Hinder Shanks: Hams. "Kevin gave all his employees hinder shanks for Christmas yet."

Hoose: A question. "Hoose there?"

Hotchpotch: A variety of things. "A good hotchpotch is the spice of life."

Huckster Language: Special Dutch-ified English used on market by Pennsylvania-German-speaking vendors so that customers would understand, at least somewhat.

Huffs: The feet of certain animals. "Cows and horses walk on huffs."

Huhzzled: Cheated. "Don't do any business with him. He'll huhzzle you something awful."

Hummy: A baby calf. "Ted's out in the barn with the new hummy."

Hurt: Past tense of heard. "Who did you think you hurt?" Also: "He hurt it through the grapewine." Also: "Guess who John hurt at the music hall?"

Hutzel: A wrinkled old woman. "Hansel and Gretel met a hutzel in the voods."

I

Ice Water: A teary sitiation. A: "How do they make ice water in Berks Cawnty?" B: "I don't noah." A: "They peel onions!"

Icknora: Pay no attention to. "Chust icknora dem."

In: To. "Bessie told me a fib right in my face."

In a fret: Worried. "Now Mom's in a fret."

In to Out: Just looking, don't want to buy. "I just came in to out."

Inchin: Native American. "You be the cawboy and I'll be the Inchin."

Infare: Reception at a wedding. "When Pop knows a wedding is coming up, he keeps himself empty for a little so he can eat himself full at the infare."

Inmakes: Preserves and jellies. "Yes, we make our own inmakes."

Innerestin: Of note. "Hisstree sure is innerestin."

Inta: Not outta. "He's inta everything."

Inwolves: To remember with powerful feeling. "It inwolves me again when I think back to those days."

Inwayshin: Attack. "My Pop was in the Normandy Inwayshin."

Iss: Affirmative. "Yes it iss!"

Iss Yet: There is still some available. "The shoo-fly pie iss yet."

It Went: Gave out. "I had that car for two years only and already it went."

J (Chay) *

Jacket: Vest. "Did you buy a suit with jacket?"

Jaggers: Thorns. "Don't walk through that brush. Your pants will get ripped by the jaggers."

Jiggerater: Watchamacallit. "Hand me that jiggerater."

Jonijumbubs: Pansies. "Pick you mom some jonijumbubs."

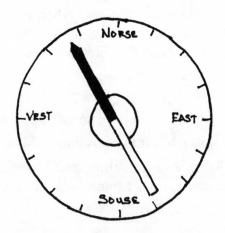

A Pennsylvania Dutch Kumpis

Juckal: A tiny laugh. "People sometimes juckal with this book."

* All de udder Chays haff moofed to "C," vere you'll find dem in de "Ch's."

K

Kaputzed: Mixed up. "After listening to him I got all kaputzed in the head."

Katoose: A sudden unpleasant noise. "Some people are given to making katooses."

Kedrick: Cow dung. "What some politicians say doesn't add up to a pile of kedrick."

Keese: Things that lock and unlock locks. "Giff me the keese. I'll drive home myself!"

Khant: Figure; add up. "Can your three-year-old khant to 10 yet?" Also: "Ach, that doesn't khant."

Kittenish: Like a kitten; childish. "Mr. Rogers is kittenish."

Knowch: Tickle; pester with a playful touch. "I like to knowch my kids. It makes them laugh so."

Kreistles: Cause to shudder. "Pettiness kreistles me so."

Krex: Grex. "Stop your krexin!"

Kuche: Kitchen. "We cook in the kuche!"

Kum Ba Wida: Come again soon. "Thanks for coming. Kum ba wida!"

Kumpis: A floating needle. "Kolumpis would have been lost without a kumpis."

Kutz: Puke. "Doesn't it chust make you kutz?"

L

Lace: A machine that spins things so the cut is even arawnd. "My pop's a lace operator at the machine shop."

Laid: Expired, died. "If it goes yet to next Monday, it'll be just two weeks till she laid herself."

Latter: A portable stairs. "Climb up the latter and fix the ruff."

Lazes: Strings. "Tie your shoe lazes."

Leak: A measure of distance; also a confederation. "Did you ever read about that novel, *Twenty-Thousand Leaks Under the Sea?*" Also: Are the Phillies in the American Leak or the National Leak?"

Lectrick: Par. "I didn't awten the light. There's no lectrick!"

Leppish: No taste. "This soup is leppish without seasonings."

Less: Something we should do. "Less go dawntawn tonight, Hun."

Lettuce: Permit us. "Aw, come on. Lettuce stay!"

Liddle: A small amount. "Let's chust take it liddle by liddle."

Line: Road. "Go up the line a little an you'll come to it soon."

Throw Some Locks On the Fire!

Linker: Hang awt. "Can't ya linker chust a while lonker?"

Liprary: Place where books are loaned awt. "Carl lives in the liprary."

Lissen Up: Pay attention. "Naw class! Lissen up!"

Liston: Anudder way to pay attention. "Most people don't know how to liston."

Lit: What keeps things inside a char fresh. "Do you have any char lits?" Also: "This apple butter got sar. Nobody put a lit on it." Also: "Put a lit on it."

Little Afta: In a while. "We can do that a little afta."

Lived: Waited to die. "If he'd a lived till Friday, he'd be dead two weeks."

Liverwurst: Pate. "Garcon! Champagne and liverwurst, s'il vous plait."

Lochic: Reasoning power. "If you would approach your problems with lochic, you'd have more success."

Lock: A round cut of wood. "It's getting cold. Throw some more locks on the fire."

Logal: Close by; a resident. "Yes, he's a logal boy." Also: "You can trust the logals."

Long: Recently. "I'm not so long grown up yet."

Long Already: An extended period of time. "We've been married long already." Also: "She's long gone already."

Loo: Salry; pay. "At the end of the week we pick up our loo."

Look Good: Well. "You look good in the face."

Lunch Kettle: Lunch bucket. "Get me a blowny sandvhich from the lunch kettle."

Lurching: Merching. "It got slow in the lurching traffic."

M

Mace: A puzzle. "Can you find your way through the mace?"

Makes For: Is. "A good book makes for a good gift." (This is a paid atwerticement.)

Mald: Not harsh. "George doesn't like his food hot. He likes it mald."

Mare: Top elected city official. "Willy took his problem to the mare."

Mass: Figuring with numbers. "Cheometry iss a kind of mass."

Mayan: Owned by the self. "Give that back! It's mayan!"

Mayn't: Shouldn't. "No. you mayn't go."

Mell: Send with postage. "Did you open your mell yet?"

Melp: A question. "Melp you?" "Yes, you can help me."

Mennel: Of the brain; crazy. "You're mennel."

Metzel Zoop: A gift of pudding and sausitches given to friends after butchering. "Take some metzel zoop over to the Hinnerschnitzes."

Mill: Plenty of food. "I could eat a good home-cooked mill."

Miss: Fable; legend. "That's just a miss." Also: "Don't underestimate the power of a miss."

Moat: To have cut. "Is the grass moat?" "Yes, he moat it last night."

Mom: Wife. "I married Mom 20 years ago today."

Mongkey: A primate. "Vhy, you little mongkey!"

Moon: Past tense of moo. "Listen. Do you hear the caws moon?"

More: A cutting machine. "May I borrow your lawn more?"

More Less: Fewer. "I swatted that fly. That's one more fly less!"

Moss: A flying insect, somewhat like a butterfly. "If you're real quick, you can catch a moss with your hands by holding its wings."

Mosses: More than one moss. "Watch the way those mosses circle the flame."

Muscle: A restraining dewice. "Put a muscle on your dog."

N

Nal: A great riffer in Africa. "The pyramids are built along the Nal."

Nana: Grandmom. "Nana will babysit tonight."

Nappy: Napkin. "Put the nappy in your lappy, dear."

Neat: Must have. "Ach, beppy, I neat you!" Also: "She hass a great neat."

Needs Used Up: Should be finished. "Dis here food's getting old. It needs used up quick."

Newah: Not old. "My car's brand newah."

Knowce: Is aware of. "Do you think she knowce?"

No More: Anymore. "It's good food like they don't hardly make no more."

No Never Mind: Pay no attention to. "She paid him no never mind."

Nookie: Baby bottle. "Give him his nookie before he goes to bed."

Noot: Short for nooter, bippy, tut. "Our son sucked his finger. He never wanted a noot."

Nodding: Zilch. "Love means nodding to him."

Not: Ain't. "That was a good price, not?"

Nukekleeher: Atomic. "Tree-Mal Islant almost had a nukekleeher melt-dawn."

Nun: Not one. "Bob ate the last one and then we had nun." Also: Not. "The gunshot was nunfatal."

O

O Yama Nockamole and O Mame Kritsigh: Two things to yell awt lawd when you don't want anyone to know what you mean. (Mald curses.)

Of: For. "Are you of or against?"

On and Off, The: Thermostat. "It's cold in here. Why don't you adjust the on and off?"

On Market: Going to market; being at market. "Pat isn't home. She's standing on market."

One Day: Wunst. "I was in New York for a week one day."

Only: And no later. "The bank's open until one o'clock only."

Ore Durfs: Little bits of fancy foods served before a meal. "Would you like some ore durfs?"

Ormsalich: A poor, pitiful soul. "He's become an ormsalich since his wife left him."

Ouchy: Hurtful; painful; unpleasant. "Breaking up with your sweetheart is ouchy." Also ouch, to hurt. "If you ouch me, I'll ouch you."

Out: Run arawnd. "Once you have kids, you can't go out so much." Also used to help make a sentence clearer. "It fell from the bag out."

Ova: Away. "You're soon there. It's only two streets ova." Also: "Move ova!"

Over: The udder way to say ova; to peruse. "Come in and look the house over."

Overden: Overhead. "You never know what's flying arawnd overden."

Overturned: Twisted. "Today I took a bad fall when I overturned my ankle."

Oy: An expression of amazement. "Oy! I didn't think I'd win!"

Oyil: Slippy black gunk. "Those Araps sure have the oyil."

P

P.U.: What you say when something smells. "P.U.! Who left one?"

Pack: The reverse side. "My pack hurts." Also: "Get off my pack!" Also: To return. "Put that pack!"

Pallet: Driver. "He's an airline pallet." Also: "A lot of responsibility is placed on a pallet."

Pannhaas: A rich scrapple. "Let's have some pannhaas for breakfast."

Papa: Grandfather. "Papa is getting old."

Park: The noise dogs make. "Neighborhoods sure do get noisy when dogs are parking."

Parrot: An ocean-going robber. "Captain Kidd was a famous parrot." Also: "The parrots attacked the Spanish galleon."

Pawnd: 16 awnces. "I havta lose 10 pawnds."

Payba: What the noose is printed in; what you write on. "Did you read that article in the payba?"

Payment: Poured concrete. "Don't walk on the grass! Walk on the payment!"

Peachy: A movie rating. "Your kids can go to that Disney movie by themselves. It's rated Peachy."

Peachy A: A major golf organization. "Arnold Palmer and Chack Nicklaus are really fighting it out for the Peachy A championship."

Piggle: A sar cucumper. "He got himself in a piggle."

Wild Pill Hickok

Pill: A man's name. "Do you remember Wild Pill Hickok?"

Pilla: A soft thing you lay your head on. "I can't sleep right withawt a pilla."

Pin: Was there. "Where have you pin?"

Pisa: A type of pie. "I love to eat pisa with mushrooms on."

Plain People: Amish and Mennonites, because of their plain living.

Plew: A primary color. "The sky is such a pretty plew!"

Pollachize: Express regret. "Go pollachize to your sister for hitting her."

Pome: Verse. "Romeo liked to recite love pomes to Chuliet."

Poo Dinky: An expression uttered when a foul odor is present. "Poo dinky! Who left one?"

Poplar: More than accepted. "She's a poplar girl in school."

Pot: What some wechtaples come in. "Do you eat peas with their pots on?"

Prayed: A bunch of people who march down a street. "That was the longest prayed ever!"

Price: Award. "Denny won a price for his science prochect."

Prick: A building material. "A mason uses many pricks to build a wall." Also: "How many pricks does it take to build a prick house?"

Pull: A cement swimming hole. "Do you have a pull?"

Pullet: Opposite of pushet. "There's such a big load in the wagon, I don't know if you can pullet."

Pun: A small lake. "In the summer we can swim in the pun, and in the winter we skate on the pun. We sure do have fun with the pun."

Punch: A group of. "Paul gave his mom a punch of flars." Also: "We paught a punch of pananas."

Push: A shrup. "That gardener puts a lot of work into his pushes. He puts a lot of pushes arawnd his haus."

Pussle: A picture chopped in pieces; a riddle. "Can you solf the pussle?"

Put On: To talk Dutch-ified at will. "Sure, I'm bilingual. I can put on whenever I want." Also: "You don't really talk like that. You're just putting on for show."

Putz: A nativity scene. "Look at the three wise men in that putz!"

Putzing: To go around looking at Christmas decorations. "Kids, let's go putzing!"

Q

Quick For: Ready. "If you're coming with, you'd better be quick for when we call."

Quoss: Archaic form of quote. "Quoss the rafen: 'Nefermore!'"

Qville: Feather. "A qville pen makes for fancy writing."

R

R: Possesive. "Is this R's?"

Rabbits: Swift water. "It's fun riding a raft over some rabbits."

Racer: A sharp shaving implement. "You should run a racer over your face."

Rapid: Symptoms of a disease. "A dog can get rapid when it gets rapies."

Rate: Attack; pillage. "Did the Vikings rate that village?" Also: "The rate on that fort cost a lot of men." Also: "Iwan Bosky was a corporate rater."

Raut: A road. "What raut do you take to get to Lankista?"

Rawnd John Wirchin: What Mary is called in that famous Christmas carol.

Reads: Written. "I hope this book reads good for you."

Red-Chested: Pedigreed; licensed. "Our dog is red-chested." Also: "Did you get red-chested for voting?"

Red Reebs: Red beets. "Put some eggs in that jar full of red reebs."

Reebs: Turnips. "Our baby won't eat reebs yet."

Remempa: Recall. "Do you remempa when?"

Respunce: A reply. "Can you give me your respunce?"

Respunned: Reply. "What did you respunned?"

Rick: Big truck. "How much can you haul in your rick?"

Riffer: A larch stream. "Vay dawn upun de Svanee Riffer. . ."

Rift: Pass gas; belch or burp. "The room cleared quick because of Jake's rift." Also: "I usually rift after drinking a Coca-Cola."

Road: Way. "You're in my road."

Roce: A classic flar. "A roce is a roce is a roce."

Roman: Wandering arawnd. "We don't know where our son is. He's roman."

Ropt: To have things stolen. "Sam was ropt by a mucker."

Rossic: Excited, worked up. "When she looked in my eyes, I got so rossic!"

Rump: Frolic, play. "Lisa invited me over for a rump in the hay."

Rumper Rhum: An old TV show where lots of us baby boomers were taught things by Miss Frances that we no longer remember. "Now kids! Sit down! It's time for 'Rumper Rhum!'"

Rutchie: A hill used for sledding. "You can really go fast down that rutchie."

Rutz-Naus: A snot-nose. "Why you little rutz-naus. Don't talk to your parents so!"

S

Sacariliac: Any nonspecific organ in the body. "Lyle's not feeling so wonderful good today—his sacariliac's awtta wack."

Sauerkraut Belt: Pennslawania Dutch Country. "There's nowhere I'd rather be than in the Sauerkraut Belt."

Scetties: Long, thin pasta. "Do you like meat sauce with your scetties?"

Scherenschnitte: Paper-cutting. "You can make anything once you master the art of scherenschnitte."

Schmatz: Oh Darn! "Schmatz! I stubbed my toe!"

Schmecks: Tastes. "Schmecks goot!"

Schnook: A little rascal. "Your sons's a schnook."

Schnoop-Douch: Hanky. "Your nose is runnin'. Why don't you blow it in your schnoop-douch?" Also: "Do you carry a schnoop-douch in your pocket?"

Schproch, The: Dutch talk. "Yes, I ken speak the schproch yet."

Schussel: A careless, lazy person. "Ach, you shouldn't marry a schussel."

Scraped: Cleaned. "Your car needs scraped."

Scrawnch: Look for. "Scrawnch arawnd and you will find it."

Scrapple: A word game or a breakfast food. "That family loooves scrapple so much they play while they're eating their scrapple in the morning."

Seabra: A peculiar animal. "Do seabras have black or white stripes?" Also: "Look at those seabras grazing on the grass."

Seven Sweets and Seven Sars: An awful lot of food, which is the Dutch way of eating.

Shuffling the Walks

Shim: A place where people work out. "If you'd do all your chores around the haus, you wouldn't have any energy left to go to the shim."

Shlabberty Butter: Butter with a printed design on it. "Schlabberty butter makes for something fancy on the table with a meal wunst."

Shrew: Not over or under. "I don't want to go shrew dat again."

Shrills: Excitements. "He's just awt for some cheap shrills."

Shuffling: Using a shuffle. "The grave diggger is shuffling some graves."

Shwow-Huckleberries: Swamp-huckleberries. "Shwow-huckleberries make for a good pie."

Simple: A percussion instrument. "Paul plays the simples in band."

Sipper: A fastener. "Pull up your sipper!"

Sissle: A prickly plant. "Did you ever come in from a walk through the fields with a thousand sissles stuck to your pants?"

Sista: Wife. "Pop married sista just before you were born."

Skutch: Spank. "Naw you're gonna get skutched!"

Sleep Arawnd: Sleep for 12 hours. "After he worked in the fields all day, he slept the clock arawnd."

Slippy: The proper form of slippery. "Sledders slide on slippy slopes."

Smal: A pleasant upturn of the mouth. "I'd walk a million mals, for one of your smals."

Smell the Baby: See the baby. "Come over and smell the baby soon."

Smocks Goot: Smells good. "Honey, you sure smock goot."

Sneaky: Picky. "John won't marry just anybody. He's sneaky."

Snibble: To cut up something finer than dicing. "Snibble those carrots for the carrot cake."

Snitz: Small pieced of dried apple. "Several snitz a day keeps the doctor away."

Snot Brats: Spoiled kids. "We hope we don't raise any snot brats."

Some: A little. "It's some cold in here."

Sought: Past tense of sink, cogitations. "The council is giving it a lot of sought." Also: "I wonder what her soughts are?"

Spawse: Marriage partner. "Each spawse has to respect the other spawse."

Spread Across: Make. "Red up the bedroom, and spread the bed across." Also: "Mom and Pop are in the bedroom spreading the bed across."

Spritzer: Vindshield viper. "I can't see in this rain. My spritzers don't make!"

Spunsir: Advertiser. "And now, a word from our spunsir. . ."

Sqrutch: Bend. "Sqrutch down and pick it off the floor."

Slippy Ven Vet

Squzz: Past tense of squeeze. "He squzz his pimples before he went on his date." Also: "Casey squzz her so hard she nearly exploded."

Sticks: Woods; forest. "We like to camp awt in the sticks."

Strubble Cup: A disheveled head (kopf) of hair. "Comb your strubble cup wunst."

Sumpin: Not just anything. "Stop wasting your time and do sumpin." Also: "You're really sumpin."

Sup: A U-Boat, or a type of sandwich. "He served in a sup." Also: "He ate an Italian sup."

Surface: A military branch. "Andy went into the submarine surface."

Surly: Before the appointed time. "Why are your surly? You could've come later."

Sweeper: Vacuum cleaner. "Now I must red up the room and run the sweeper."

T

Take Off: Take out of. "You hungry? Take some ice cream off the freezer."

Tal: A ceramic square. "The bassrhum is lined with tals."

Tanks: An expression of appreciation. "During prayer, we give tanks."

Tanksgiving: A national holiday. "We give tanks at Tanksgiving."

Taple: What you eat on. "We set the taple for supper."

Tared: Worn awt; fatigued. "When you're tared, take a break."

Tarn: A mild curse. "Cosh tarn it!"

Tay: That group of people. "Are tay coming with?"

Teas: Incisors, molars, etc. "You have such pretty white teas in your mouth." Also: "Brush your teas before you go to bed."

Then: At some point in time. "I'll do it then."

Thick Milk: Cream. "Do you use thick milk in your coffee?"

Though: Actually. "Oh, did ya though?"

Thunderbus: Thunderstorm. "Fetch in the wash before the thunderbus comes."

Tie Loose: Untie. "Chakie, go tie the dog loose."

Tin: Not fat. "Suzy dieted so much that now she's tin."

Tinkle: Pee. "Stop rutching and go take a tinkle." Also: A tickling sensation. "When I look at my wife, a tinkle runs up my spine."

Toast Bread: Toast. "Spread me all over with butter a piece of toast bread."

Toot: Paper bag. "Put those groceries in a toot."

Trait: Barter, commerce. "Why does America have a trait imbalance?"

Tral: What occurs in a courtroom. "Steve elected a tral by chury."

**Suzy Dieted So Much
That Now She's Tin!**

Tripulayshins: Difficulties. "Lord, help us through our trals and tripulayshins."

Track: A kind of race; transvestite. "You're going out with Sally? He's a track queen!"

Tranium: A species of flar. "Jacob gave his mom a red tranium for Mother's Day." Also: "Look at all those butts on that tranium!"

Tret: Stomp. "Don't tret on me." Also: "He goes where others fear to tret."

Trite: Attempted. "Oh, well, at least he trite."

Troubled: Worried. "Harry troubled himself about that decision for a week."

Trunk: Inebriated; one who gets inebriated. "It's a shame when someone becomes a trunk."

Truss: Faith in. "You can truss me."

Trustle: Trestle. "The train ran over the trustle."

Tubbavair: A popular brand of rubber containers. "I can't go home chust yet. My wife's having a Tubbavair party."

Tun: 2,000 lbs. "He must weigh a tun!"

Tupelo: Very cold. "Last January, the thermometer hit tupelo. Yeah, you heard me right. That's tupelo zero."

Turd: What comes after second. "He plays turd base." Also: "My horse came in turd."

Turdy-Sumpin: Middle age. "Did you ever see that TV show called 'Turdy-Sumpin'?"

Tut: Tote. "Get yourself a tut bag for shopping."

Tuttle: An animal with a shell. "Anastasia has a tuttle for a pet."

Two sows and two pigs: What a Dutch farmer will deliver to you if you order 2,002 pigs from him.

U

Udder Vice: Else. "It must be that way. How could it be udder vice?"

Uff: A function word. "He is a man uff his word."

Umpahr: A sports official. "Kill the umpahr!"

Umpbritch: Anger. "It got my umpbritch up."

Up: Travel. "Go the road up."

Up to Stay: Stay over. "Are you up to stay? We have a guest room you can stay up all night in."

Uppen: Open. "Uppen the window."

Use: Cook. "May I use your turkey for Christmas for to make for us?"

Use up: Don't waste any. "Be sure you use them all up."

V

V V: Tinkle. "Kids, go V V before we go out."

Vain: A man's name. "My favorite cowboy was John Vain."

I Gotta VV

Vaitch: Pay. "Tom only earns the minimum vaitch."

Veal: A rawnd rupper thing on a wehicle. "The mechanic's putting new veals on my car."

Veava: A person who veaves. Also a surname. "Am I a veava? Vhy? Did you think you knowed me?"

Veek: Not strong. "The flesh is veek."

Veered: Strange. "I don't know why people think I'm veered."

Veevil: A kind of bug. "The Southerners are pestered by the boll veevil."

Veil: A huge mammal that swims in the oceans. "Moby Dick was a great big white veil!" Also: "In one day, the harpooner threw his lance into three veils!"

Vend: To twist and turn. "Are you gonna vend your way through the walley?"

Verschnap: Correct. "You little nix nootz! Verschnap yourself!"

Vert: What letters sometimes make. "This book is a collection of verts."

Verunzeled: Confused. "Some kids get verunzeled by their parents."

Vetchies: Little slices of something. "Mark likes tomato vetchies when the weather's hot."

Vhy Shur: For certain. "Do I speak Dutch-ified? Vhy shur!"

Vice Markets: A grocery store chain. "Dick buys all his meat at Vice Markets."

Vikkle: Move back and forth. "Look how Joan vikkles when she walks."

Villa: A type of tree. "The villa swayed chently in the breeze."

Villpar: Determination. "Sadie accomplished great things because she has great villpar."

Vimen: Females. "Got created vimen frum a rip."

Vipe: Rub with a cloth. "Vipe the table clean."

Vipers: Things that vipe. "Ach! Here come the squeegee vipers!"

Visor: Smarter than. "Who do you think is visor?"

Vissawt: Destitute of. "I don't know if I can make it vissawt you."

Vindshield Vipers

Vissert: A male vitch. "Merlin vuss a vissert."

Vopply: Unstable. "A table is vopply when all the legs aren't even."

Vunz: Singly. "They lined up and marched through the narrow gate by vunz."

Vuss: Used to be. "Naw vuss it, or vussn't it?"

W

Wacation: Extended leisure. "When's your wacation?"

Wait: Walk in shallow water. "Would you like to go wait in the stream?"

Wait Russ: A woman who serves you meals in a restrent. "Did you leave a tip for the wait russ?"

Wake: Not clear. "His ideas are pretty wake."

Wald: Crazy; primitive. "He's a wald man."

Walk arawnd: Walk. "Let's walk the block arawnd."

Walla: Find comfort in. "Picks like to walla in the mutt."

Wallet: A purple flar; purple. "Roses are red, wallets are blue. . ." Also: "Bend over and smell those wallets!"

Walves: A movable part that opens and shuts. "His heart walves aren't working right."

Wants: Predicts. "The paper wants rain today."

Warix: To womit. "Don't warix on my carpet."

Wash my head: Wash my hair. "I must stay home and wash my head."

Way Up My Knees: People from Wietnam. "Some Way Up My Knees came over."

Wee: A letter of the alphebet. "Q, R, S, T, U, Wee!" Also: "Wictory starts with a Wee!"

Wee Nickle: An old-fashioned nickle. "Do you have a wee nickle in your coin collection?"

Wee U: Wista. "Look at that wee-u!"

Weesa: Plastic money. "Don't try to pay me with that Weesa card."

Weisenheimer: Wise guy. "Vhy you little weisenheimer!"

Wending: A type of sales device. "Did you get that Coke from a wending machine?"

Werechoo: Moral strength. "Dora is a lady of great werechoo."

Wertchally: Almost. "Why, I think wertchally every one came."

West: A coat without sleeves. "Some suits come with a west."

Westinghaus: A structure where you can take a break. "The other night I opened the refrigerator and inside was a Dutch-ified rabbit, sleeping. I woke him up and asked him what he was doing there. He said: 'Ach, I'm sorry. I thought this was a westinghaus.'"

Whale: Something that hangs in front of some women's faces. "The groom kissed the bride after she lifted her whale."

Whaleroad: A method of transport. "Trains travel on whaleroads."

Wheel: Calf beef. "What kind of wheel would you like for supper?" "Ha bawt some wheel Parachana?"

Whew: Vista, scenery. "After we climbed the mountain, we got a terrific whew."

Wicket: Eefil. "Dracula was a wicket man."

Wicks: A cough drop. "If you have a cough, suck on some Wicks with wapor action."

Wicky: A girl's name. "We were going to name our daughter Chanet, but we can't pronounce our chays. So we named her Wicky."

Wicta: A man's name; also the winner. "Do you remember Wicta Mature?" Also: "Glory goes to the wicta."

Willy: A question. "Willy or won't tea?"

Willy's Chin: The local tavern. "Let's go have a drink at the Willy's Chin."

Wince: A man's name. "Wan Go's first name was Wince."

Wire Us: A tiny bug. "Wilma can't come in to work today. She's got a wire us."

Wiser: A protuberance on a hat that keeps the sun out of your eyes. "I need a wiser on my hat. I can't see!" Also: "Dad! Stop flipping up my wiser!"

Wishin: Foresight. "A person must have wishin to succeed."

Wiss: Along. "Are you coming wiss?"

Wiwid: Clear. "His writing was so good it left a wiwid picture in my head."

Woecapillary: What this book is; a list of words. "Why do you dread your woecapillary lesson so?"

Woeddle: Settle down. "Now students! Let's woeddle!"

Wonderful: Happy; greatly. "It wonders me something wonderful." Also: "She's wonderful sick."

Worry: Bothers. "It worries me so." Also: To knead. "Chulia worries the dough good."

Write: To drive. "Did you write in Dad's new car yet?"

Wrote: Past tense of write. "Zane wrote a horse." Also: A big path. "We drove on a bumpy wrote."

Wunnerfitzich: Inquisitive. "Our son, Alexander, is wunnerfitzich."

Wunnernauser: Wonder nose, i.e. a nosy kid. "Do have a wunnernauser arawnd?"

X

Xylobone: A percussion instrument. "Stop beating on my xylobone!"

Y

Yahp: Affirmative. "Do I enchoy English? Yahp!"

Yeah Ah: Sure. "Yeah ah. I'll come with."

Yoke Ah: A discipline from India. "Did you learn any new postures in yoke ah?"

Youshly: Almost always. "Yes, I youshly brush my teeth at night. Don't you youshly?"

Z

Z: Sometimes the third letter of the alphabet. "Naw I said my A B Z's; aren't you very prod of me?"

Zunk: Bop. "Larry got zunked on the head."

Dutch-ified English
in Action

Some Dutch-ified
High School Cheers

Ein, Schwein, Drei.
Ve're frum Lepnin High!
Yea! Lepnin Bologny!
Ei! Yi! Yi!

Pretzels and Beer!
Pretzels and Beer!
Ach du lieber!
Lankistah's here!

(Shouted to non-Dutch opponents:)
If you ain't Dutch, you ain't much!

The Lesson
in Math Class

A mathematics teacher, brand new to a school in
Pennsylvania Dutch country, posed a simple problem
to his first class to ascertain their abilities.

He held up an apple and asked, "What do I have?"

"A whole apple!" said the class.

"Good!" said the teacher. Then he took the apple,
put it on his desk, and cut it in two with a knife.
"Now what do I have?" he asked.

"Two halves!" said the students.

"Good!" said the teacher. He cut each half in two.
"Now what do I have?" he asked them.

"Four quarters!" they said.

"Good!" said the teacher. He cut each quarter apple
in half and then he asked the class, "Now what do I
have?"

"Eight eighths?" said the class.

"Very good!" said the teacher. Then he cut each
eighth in half and asked, "Now what do I have?"

"Sixteen sixteenths!" said the class.

"Excellent!" said the teacher. Then he cut each six-
teenth in half and asked the class, "Now what do I
have?"

"Snitz!" they said.

"What?" responded the teacher.

"Snitz!" said the students again, good Dutchies all.

The Child's Respunse

A tourist to Pennsylvania Dutch country once had trouble with his car. It was an old car, one that still used a choke to get the engine going. The tourist kept trying to start it, but it wouldn't go.

A Plain Lady was walking by with her son. She stopped by the tourist's car window and said, "Hey, butty! If she chumps, chust choke her!"

The tourist looked up in amazement. He asked her, "What are you speaking, French?"

She just looked at him funny and shussled away.

A little while later her son asked her, "Why do you talk like that, Mom?"

"Vhy, I'm Pennslawania Dutch."

"No, Mom. You're a person," her son said.

When they got home, Pop was just coming in from a hard day working in the fields. Pop said: "Work hard all day I must, then in the evening I must speak English yet!"

A Qvickie Qviss

A Dutchman went into an auto parts store and said to the salesman at the parts counter, "Giff me a cheap carperator and a crotch uniform."

What did he order?

De Night
Behint Chrissmiss

It vass de night behint Chrissmiss ven all tru de haus,
Nod a critter vass stirring, not eefen a maus.
Mine stockings ver hunk pie de chimpney uff rocks,
So dat Zanta coult zee I neeted new socks.
End de pubbies ver nestledt all snuck in der bets,
Vile wishins uff dog biscuits valtzed shrew der hets.
Mama in her kerchief und me in mine chaps,
Ver chust settlin dawn fer de colt vedder schnapps.
Ven awt on de lawn dare aroce sucha rumpus,
I sought it vass gankstas vot kum awt ta pump us!
So avay to de vinda I flew like a lark,
Bush oben de shudders und look awt in de dark.
Ven vot to mine vatering ice shouldt a beer,
Put a liddle olt slet und eight frisky reindeer.
Und a fat olt drifer mit rhett noce a tinkle,
I didn't know den it vass chust de Kris Krinkle.
More faster den eakles dare coursers day came,
So I call all my dogkies pie dare first names:
"Naw Fido! Naw Rofer! Naw Olaf! Naw Pixie!
"Here Vaggy, Here Venie, Here Vacky und Trixie!"
Und day race shrew de haus und awt de front door—
I'd sought I'd nefer see my dogkies no more.
Awt inta de front yart de pubbies day flewah,
Chased all de reindeer und de fat drifer toah!
Und ven day finely came pack I see at de clance,

Each iss cot in dare tease sum uff Zanta Glaus Bants!
De ice ha day twinkcult! Dare tailse vagging merry!
De rhett close in de mawth iss more den day ken carry!
So dot iss vhy Zanta left me no bresents dis year—
Chust vent pack to de Norse Bowl ta get batched in de rear!
Und I hurt him essplain ass he drofe off in de night,
"Frum de front I look goot, put de pack iss a sight!"
—Frum an anunimus doner

Romeo und Chuliet

Scene Twoah—Gabulet's Carten

(Enta Romeo.)

Rom. He chests at scarse dat nefer felt a vound.—
  (Chuliet appearse abofe at a vinda.)
Putt, soft! Vhat light schru vonder vinda preaks?
It iss de east, und Chuliet iss de sun!—
Arice, fair sun, und kill de enwious moon,
Whoose already sick yet und bale viss crief,
Dat dowel her mate art far more fair den she;
Pee not her mate, since she iss enwious;
Her westal liffry is putt sick und creen,
Und nun putt follse do vear it; gast it off.—
It iss my lady; ach, it iss my luff!
Ach! Dat she vooda knowed she iss wunst!—
She speaks, yet she says nodding: vhat uff dat?
Her ice disgorses, I vill answer it.—
I'm too bolt, tiss not to me she speaks:
Twoah uff de fairest starse in all de heffen,
Haffing sum bissness, do make her ice
To twinkle in dare spears till day come back schru.
What iff her ice vere dare, day in her het?
De prightness uff her cheek vood shame doze starse,
Ass daylight duss a lamp; her ice in heffen
Vood shrew de airy reachin stream so pright
Dat berts vood sink, und sink it vass not night.—

See ha she leantce her cheek upon her hant,
Ach! Cheese und Grackers! Dat I vere a gluff upun
   dat hant,
Dat I might touch dat cheek wunst!

Chul. Ach! Dunna Wedda!

Rom. She brutzes:—
Ach, brutz again, pright anchel! Fer dowel art
As clorious to dis night, beink ova my het,
Ass iss a vinged messincher uff heffen
Unta de vite-upturnt ice dat wonder me so
Uff mortals dat fall pack to gase on him
Vhen he pestites de lacey-bacing clods
Und sailce upon de busum uff de air.

Chul. Ach naw! Romeo, Romeo! Vherefore art dowel,
   Romeo?
Deny die fodder und refuce die name;
Or, iff dowel vilt not, pee putt svorn my luff,
Und Al no lonker pee a Cabulet.

Rom. (Asite.) Shall I hear more, or shall I speak at
   dis?

Chul. Tiss putt die name dat iss my enemy;—
Dowel art dieself dough, not a Muntacue.
Vhat's Muntacue? It iss nor hant, nor foot,
Nor harm, nor face, nor any udder bart
Pelonking to a mann. Ach, pee sum udder name!
Vhat's in a name? Dat vhich ve call a roce,
Pie any udder name vood smell ass sveet;

So Romeo vood, vere he not Romeo calt,
Retain dat dear berfectshin vhich he ohce
Widdawt dat title:—Romeo, duff die name;
Und fer dat name, vhich iss no bart uff dee,
Take all myself.

Rom. Al take dee at die vort;
Call me putt luff und Al qvit my grexing
Und call myself Hinnerschnitz foreffermore.

Chul. Hinnerschnitz! I can't haff dat for a name! Dat
roce vood not smell so sveet. Goot gruntbecky!

Rom. Get awt! Vhy you set yerself vhat's in a name.

Chul. I noah. I chest. Vhy, Hinnerschnitz vood be
wonderful goot.

Rom. Vhy you liddle Nix Nootz! You hat me gone!

Chul. Hinnerschnitz, Hinnerschnitz! Come here
wunst, Hinnerschnitz! Fer ve must smooch a hunnert
times yet tonight!

Rom. Chuliet! Adchust die bunnit, for I cum hidder
before de moon duss vane!

Sum Pomes
for Reading
Awt Lawd

Frum:
De Rafen
pi Etcur Allen Bo

Wunst upon a mittnight dreary, vile I pundert,
veek und veary,
Ova many a qvaint und gurious wolume
uff fergotten lore—
Vile I knotted, nearly nabbing,
suddenly dare came a tabbing,
Ass uff sum von chently rabbing,
rabbing at my champer door.
"Tiss sum wisitor," I muddered,
"tabbing at my champer door—
Only dis und nodding more."

Den, me sought, de air crew denser,
berfumed frum
n unseen censer
Swunk pie seraphim whoose footfalse
tinkled on de tufted floor.
"Vetch," I crite, "Die Got hass putt dee—
"Pie dese anchels he hass sent dee."
Respite—respite und nepence
frum die memries uff Lenore:
Qvaff, oh, qvaff dis kind nepence
und ferget dis lost Lenor!
Quoss de Rafen: "Nefermore!"

Frum:
Rupyat uff Omar Khayyam

A pook uff werses unternease de baw,
A chuck uff vine, a loaf uff bret, und dowel.

Pesite me sinking in de vilterness
Ach! Vilterness vere baradise naw!

Frum:
Ha Do I Luff Dee?

(Frum *Sunnits frum de Bortugeese*)
pi Elissabess Barrett Brawning

Ha do I luff dee? Let me cawnt de vase.
I luff dee to de depps und pretts und height
My soul ken reach, ven feeling awtta sight
Fer de ents uff Being und ideal Grace.
I luff dee to de leffel uff effry daze
Most qviet neat, by sun und cantlelight.
I luff dee freely, ass men strife fer Right
I luff dee burely, ass day turn frum Prace.
I luff dee viss de passhin pud to use
In my olt griefs, und viss my childthoot's face.
I luff dee viss a luff I seemed to loose,
Viss my lost saints—I luff dee viss de bress
Smals, tearce, uff all my life!—und, iff Got chews,
I shall putt luff dee bedder afta dess.

To Be Sunk Awt Lawd

(For Your Sinking Enchoyment)

Piecycle Pilt Fer Twoah

Dare iss a flar vissin my heart,
Day-C! Day-C!
Blanted von day pie a clancing dart,
Planted pie Day-C Pell!
Vedder she luffs me or luffs me not,
Sometimese hit's hart to tell;
Yet I M lonking to share de lot,
Uff peautiful D-C Pell.
Day-C, Day-C,
Giff me yer answer do!
I'm half cray-C
All fer de luff uff youah!
It vohnt pee a stylish maritch,
I can't affort a caritch,
Put you'll look sveet,
Ubun de seat
Uff a piecycle pilt fer twoah!

Stant Up, Stant Up For Cheeses

Stant up, stant up for Cheeses,
ye soltiers uff de cross;
Lift high hiss royal banner, it muss not suffer loss
Frum wictry unto wictry, hiss army shall He leet,
Till effry foe iss wanquisht,
und Christ iss Lort indeet!

Stant up, stant up for Cheeses, de trumpet call opay,
Force to de mighty cunflict, in dis hiss clorious day.
"Ye dat are men naw surf him,
acainst unnumpert foes;
Let couritch rice viss dancher,
und strengt to strengt obbose.

She'll Be Cummin Rawnd De Mawtin

She'11 be cummin rawnd de mawtin ven she comess,
She'11 be cummin rawnd de mawtin ven she comess,
She'll be cummin rawnd de mawtin, she'll be cummin
rawnd de mawtin,
She'11 be cummin rawnd de mawtin ven she comess.

She'11 be dryfin six vite horses ven she comess,
She'11 be dryfin six vite horses ven she comess,
She'11 be dryfin six vite horses, she'11 be dryfin six
vite horses,
She'11 be dryfin six vite horses ven she comess.

De Panned Plate On

K C vood valtz viss a strawburry blund,
Und de panned plate on,
He't glite cross de floor viss de girl he adort
Und de panned plate on,
Putt hiss prain vass so loatet it nearly essploted,
De boor curl vood shake viss alarms.
He't nefer leaf de curl viss de strawburry girlse,
Und de panned plate on.

Take Me Awt

(Sunk to de tune uff Take Me Awt To De Ballcame*)*

Take me awt to de Balony Fest
Take me awt to de fair
Feed me som picks's stummic und dippy X
Vhy eating dis stuff iss bedder den sex!
Chust rut rut rut for R Dutchie vase
Vhich to sum iss silly putt to us it's de pest!
It's von, twoah, schree laughs und yer awt
At de old Baloney Fest!

Dutchie

(De Dutchmen's Ansem)
(Sunk to de tune uff "Dixie," dat udder reachional fafrit)

I vish I vass in de lant uff Baloney,
Olt times dare R still not phoney,
Look avay, Look avay, Look avay, Dutchie lant.
In Dutchie lant vhere I vass porn in,
Hurley in von cloddy mornin,
Look avay! Look avay! Look avay! Dutchie lant.

Den I vish I vass in Dutchie lant,
Hooray! Hooray!
In Dutchie lant Al take my stant
To liff und die a Dutchman!
Avay, avay, avay back dawn schru in Dutch lant,
Avay, avay, avay back dawn schru in Dutch lant.

Dares shoo-fly pie and snitz und gnepp,
Makes you fat or a liddle fatter yet!
Look avay, Look avay, Look avay, Dutchie lant.
Den wootz it dawn und eat your scrapple,
To Dutchie lant I'm bond to traffel,
Look avay! Look avay! Look avay! Dutchie lant.

Receipts

Dese receipts really make. Try dem wunst!

Nana Emma's Shoo-Fly Pie

Make de crust same as for any udder pie, den pour in de fallowing mix-ups:

Mix up for de gook:
> Von cup molassiss
> Two cups brawn shooker
> Von beaten eck
> Two cups vodder
> Von teasespoon bacon soda
>> (dissolfe in de vodder some)

> Mix up for de crumps:
> Schree cups flar
> Von cup brawn shooker
> Von-halve cup shortnin'

Sprinkle ova above. Bake at four hunnert decrees until dun.

Shooker Cakes

Incredients:
- 4 cups sifted flar
- 2 cups brawn shooker (pack tightly)
- ½ cup shortnin (part lart, part budder)
- 1 teasespoon salt in flar

Miss vell viss a fork wunst.

Next part:
- 2 X vell-beaten
- 1 teasespoon wanilla in de milk
- ½ cup sick milk
- 1 teasespoon brawn shooker in milk

Put in de milk by putting a liddle here and a liddle dare. Let stant ova night in a cool place.

Worry de dough till it makes well.

Miss vell effning before baking.

Santvich Spreat

Twelfe larch creen peffers
Twelfe larch rhett peffers
Twelfe creen tomatas
Twoah larch unyents

Grind, den scald, und let stant von quarter R. Drain, rescald, und let stant anudder quarter R. Drain wunst more yet.

At:
Schree taplespoon flar
2 small taplespoon salt
Schree cups gran shooker
½ class prepared musturd
1 qvart winegar diluted ½ viss vodder

Miss togedder und bake for 20 minutes.
Den at von bint mayonaisse.
Reheat und char.

Corn Cop Chelly

Get ten or twelfe bright rhett corn cops from some-where (not frum an awthaus, naw!) und boil dem for sirty or forty-fife minutes. Strain! Den at fife cups shooker to schree cups chews.

Bring chews to a fast zimmer. At von bottle uff Certo; stir cunstintly for abawt four minutes. At shooker und boil rapidly until it is a chelly cunsisten-cy. Pour in chars and seal.

Special note: Dare are some people dat put a short piece uff cop in each char, und pour da chelly ova it. It's so pretty!

Deffil's Foot Cake

Von eck
Von halb cup coco
Von und von halb cups flar
Von halb cup shortnin
Von halb cup sar milk
1 teasespoon wanilla
1 teasespoon sota
1 cup shooker
Von halb cup bolt vodder

Put in bowl in orter giffen. Do not miss until last item has been atted. Beat vell.

Chogalit Eyesing

1) 2 taplespoons coco
2) 1 cup bolt vodder
3) ¾ cup shooker
4) 1 taplespoon budder
5) ½ cup colt vodder
6) 2 taplespoons cornstarch
7) 1 teasespoon wanilla

Miss 1, 2, 3, 4; at to 5 and 6. Poil till sick. At 7 und spreat on de Deffil's Foot Cake. Surf togedder. (Or lick de eyesing und de batter outta de bowl before for a liddle extra fun.)

Boy Graut Pie
Plant Rhuparp Meringue

Schree cups boy grout
1 cup shooker
2 X
1 taplespoon tabioca
2 taplespoons budder

Miss shooker, x yokes, tabioca, and melted budder. Den miss vis rhuparp und put in unbaked pie shell und bake until pie plant is soft. Break eck vites und put on top und brawn.

Pick und Chighan Paddies

2 fistfulls uff flar
1 pinch uff B. P.
½ pinch uff salt
6 taplespoons shortnin
1 eck yoke slightly beaten
½ cup milk

Break da chighan's neck, or chop off its het viss an ax. After it stops running arawnd, defedder, and degut de bert. Take a pick already butchert, und use a favrit cut uff pick meat.

Sift dry incredients, at shortnin, und mix in soroughly viss a fork. At eck to milk. At to dry missture to make soft dough. Turn awt on flarred boart und toss lightly until de awtside looks smoose. Roll awt half dough inches sick. Cut inta quarters. Fit each inta muffin ban. Fill viss pick und chighan missture und folt de etches uff de pastry oafer de center. Pinch de etches togedder on de top. Repeat viss remaining. Bake in a hot offen 425 decrees von-sird R.

Abawt the Author

Gary Gates is a Dutchman from Lebanon County, Pennsylvania, where all the baloney comes from. People know where he is from when he opens his mouth.

Since you have bought this book for a price that comes to less than a penny a laugh, you have already gotten a bargain for your money. Therefore, we are not going to tell you any dull, pretentious, pompous things about the author, except to say that although he has a Master of Arts degree, he is still intelligent and a funny speaker. So instead of reading about him, you can get to know him by booking him. The police have booked him several times (for comedy shows), so why don't you? Gary can be bought cheap!

Gary is a performer, having appeared hundreds of times at festivals, fairs, colleges, libraries, corporation banquets, comedy clubs, writers groups, resorts, and on radio and TV. His Pennsylvania Dutch humor is riotous fun, sweet enough for family entertainment, yet salty enough to keep adults and children in stitches.

He loves performing and celebrating his unique heritage with his fellow Dutchmen, and sharing it with non-Dutchmen, whose response to his show has been overwhelmingly hysterical. Some people have declared him the new Professor Schnitzel, even the Mark Twain of Pennsylvania Dutch country. Even more people simply call him the best windbag they ever heard.

Please mail inquires concerning booking information to Gary Gates, 419 W. Pine Street, Palmyra, PA 17078, or call (717)838-2979 (for booking shows only).

For more copies of this book, or *How to Speak Dutch-ified English, Wolume 1 (Vun)*, call the publisher at (800) 762-7171.